One of the strengths of Master McShane's classroom practice is the variety: I have never experienced the same class; there is always a different mix of aerobics, strength training and martial arts drills. However, in each class the underlying principle is the same: honor the work you have done and challenge yourself to do at least a little bit better today. Most importantly, open yourself to the possibilities that can take place in your life when you are willing to push yourself past where you have ever been. This book is a necessary complement to that philosophy and I believe it is indispensable."

— Reginald Flood
Professor of English
Eastern Connecticut State University

"Dear Master McShane,

I really enjoyed Sensei Secrets. It's an insightful and comprehensive guide for Karate Mom's & Dad's. I am sure that both new parents of martial arts and "seasoned veteran" parents will benefit from reading and re-reading this book. Great Job!"

— Master Steven Voelker
Grandmaster & Founder
Pyong Hwa Kunin Tang Soo Do
and Middlesex Tang Soo Do Academy

I0202323

"I consider myself incredibly fortunate to have been a student of Sensei McShane, as well as the mother of a couple of students. I was also very lucky to be able to train with some of the young people who were fellow students of mine.

When I first met him, he was a young man who embodied every one of the characteristics that one thinks of when they think martial arts. *Respect. Discipline. Focus. Confidence. Perseverance. Humility.* As an adult student, I learned what these words really meant because of the young man who showed me what they really meant in the way he lived and the way he shared so much of himself so freely. More, I watched the children who came through the program grow to embody all these things too. I watched Sensei McShane foster a community where respect was assumed. Mostly I think because of the respect that was shown to everyone who entered the magic of Sensei McShane's dojo. At first I wondered if the youth that already had these character traits were more drawn to martial arts, and that may or may not be true, but I do know that Charlie McShane has an incredible gift in the connection he is able to make with his students.

Whatever the reason any of his students is drawn to him, they are all better people for having known him. This guide is far more than a publication to help your child with martial arts, it's a guide to helping your child get the most from life, and for you to have the best relationship you possibly can with your child. 'Sensei Secrets' should have a favored place on the bookshelf of every parent and grandparent."

— **Patti Osborne**, *Hawaii*

"I walked into the dojo in Norwich five years ago as someone who had spent almost twenty years in a classroom teaching young people to read and write – struggling to help them elevate the skills they acquired in high school into the intellectual tools that would help them succeed as students at the university level. When I began training in martial arts, I expected to be challenged physically to improve my fitness level and gain expertise in martial arts techniques that would give me confidence in my ability to defend myself. Both of those things happened in ways that exceeded my expectations, but perhaps the most unexpected gift was the exposure, class after class, to a way of teaching that creates a student-centered space that transforms lives. The philosophy that shapes the pages of this book has changed my life and the lives of my daughter and son. It is a philosophy that extends beyond the mats and the walls of the dojo to provide a method that helps me positively encourage success in all of their endeavors.

I have been to countless conferences focusing on teaching methodology, and on a regular basis I participate in workshops with colleagues on teaching methods and classroom practice. However, no activity has improved my teaching skills and brought greater focus to improving student learning than training at ABD.

The way that Master McShane blends important life lessons about commitment, integrity and perseverance into an hour immersed in rigorous exercise that challenges the body and unlocks the mind is what I strive to do in my writing classroom. The balance between drills and hands-on activities, the creative repetition of old material meshed with new techniques, and a quiet insistence on a student's best effort is what I strive to duplicate in my college writing classroom.

SENSEI SECRETS FOR MOM & DAD

A PARENT'S GUIDE TO HELPING YOUR CHILD

GET THE MOST FROM THE MARTIAL ARTS

Charlie McShane

Sensei Secrets for Mom & Dad

Copyright © 2012 by Charlie McShane
Second Edition 2016

Cover photo by Randy Gallogly
Photos by Xavier Dunn

Formatting and Design by Pedro Daddario

All rights reserved. No part of this book may be reproduced or transmitted in any form or by any means without written permission from the author.

DEDICATION

Formatting/Design

Many thanks to Pedro Daddario for voluntarily formatting this second printing, spending countless hours making it look as it does, offering suggestions, and dealing with my often delayed answers. He had some great ideas for things I would have never thought of. And did I mention it was voluntary?

Family

Wife Kristin, Daughter Annie, Mom, Dad, Brother Marc, and Sister Megan.

Instructors

Master Steven Voelker, Master Ken Jacobs, Master Steve Daum, Master Dave Bloomquist at *Middlesex Tang Soo Do*.
Master Paul Garcia and the *America's Best Defense* team.
Bill Montgomery and Joan Love at *Norwich Judo*.
Brad Wolfson and Marcio Stambowsky at *Gracie Sports*.

Students

Josh Hesser, Kayla Fritz, Angel Ayala, and the thousands of students who have come through the doors of my little dojo in the last ten years. I've learned the most about teaching from you.

CONTENTS

1 WHY MARTIAL ARTS?

There's a reason you're here, reading this little book. You want to help your child excel in this new activity.

But first, let me ask: why martial arts? Did you bring your child with goals in mind? Something specific, like focus or respect? Is self-defense a concern, or do you just want to fill the time between baseball and soccer? Maybe to find a new competitive outlet?

Parents initially enroll their kids in martial arts for a number of purposes—but they *keep* them in martial arts for bigger, better reasons, once they see the profound and life-changing effects that diligent practice can provide. This book is designed to assist you in helping your "Karate Kid" get the most from the study of martial arts.

Although I may not know you, in my twenty-plus years teaching martial arts to children I've certainly known parents like you. The fact that you're taking the time to read this book qualifies you as a supportive and involved Karate Parent. I'm excited to help you navigate through the ups—and yes, downs—of martial arts training for your child.

The book is broken down into chapters by attaching character qualities to different belt colors. In truth, these mental attributes do not always show up in this order. For that matter, your dojo may not use the same belt order presented in this book. I've laid out the chapters this way because this is the sequence I often see young martial artists mature through.

Training is good for everyone, but...

> *Martial arts is concerned with one thing: personal improvement.*

I believe all children can benefit from martial arts lessons—boys, girls, athletic, uncoordinated, outgoing, shy, ADHD, Asperger's, and so on.

Personally, I see the dojo as a "safe-haven" physical pursuit, especially well adapted to children who have *not* excelled in team sports.

I have nothing against team sports. For some kids, they are extremely worthwhile but—having been a child whose experiences in baseball and soccer were challenging at best, damaging at worst—I can say that there's a place in the dojo for everyone.

In the martial arts, you're not compared to others like you can be in competitive sports. There's no bench to "warm." You progress at your own pace, and strengths are uncovered with time and effort.

There's no scoreboard, no shot clock, no drafting. Taught correctly by a caring instructor, your child will only be judged against his or her potential. In short, the competition is within yourself, not against anyone else.

There is a competitive aspect to martial arts training, but it is only that—one aspect of many. Tournaments have their place but aren't for everyone. Your Sensei will know if this activity is right for your child.

Before we start, a few general guidelines that will make your role as a black belt parent easier for you and more rewarding for your child...

SENSEI SECRETS

7 PARENT DO'S AND DON'TS

1. Do be involved. Stay, watch class, pay attention. Practice with them at home. Your child can sense your commitment to their training.

2. Don't be a drop-off parent! Good dojos have seating sections. Use them!

3. Do praise effort before you seek results! As you'll read in chapter one, progress is a process!

4. Don't compare! As mentioned, all kids are different. Using phrases like *better than* or *worse than* are not healthy within the dojo.

5. Do use martial arts training, culture, and lessons to influence your child's behavior outside of the dojo. Reminding them to conduct themselves with *black belt discipline* in the supermarket can be very effective!

6. Don't threaten to take away classes for bad behavior. Remember why you brought them to the dojo in the first place. You wouldn't say "No more school until your spelling improves!"

7. Do realize that the mental aspects of martial arts, in many ways, are no different from the physical ones. Your child will have to practice the same roundhouse kick thousands and thousands of times to become *black belt level*.

Like kicks, the qualities of focus, respect, and self-control are consciously practiced thousands of times before they become habit. Just as it takes time, coaching, and repetition to develop the coordination and balance to execute that kick expertly—it takes just as much determination to internalize the mental aspects.

Your Sensei will tell you that the perfect roundhouse kick is never attained. No matter how many years you practice, you can always get a little better.

A martial artist pursues perfection, knowing that it will never happen. Please remember this when observing your Karate Kid—success is not measured by perfection and we grow by inches, not miles.

It's my goal with this book to help you provide the best martial arts experience for your child, but also to convince you that martial arts training is a lifestyle concerned with one thing: personal improvement.

And now, onto the most important belt and concept of all...

2 WHITE BELT

CONFIDENCE

Congratulations, your child is a martial artist! This is a historic time, so be sure to take lots of pictures! Did you know that every black belt—every one—was a once a white belt? This marks the first step in a thousand mile journey of improvement, goal setting, and self-realization.

Of course, your child doesn't care about all that philosophical stuff. Not your kid, running around the yard kicking everything he shouldn't be. Time honored traditions of self-improvement through continuous study, challenge, and achievement? No way! I just want to "Ninja Turtle" everything in my path!

Don't worry, Mom. It's okay, Dad. Given time, your little white belt will outgrow this phase and, with nurturing and skilled instruction, will one day embody all the qualities you hope for. It just takes a little while, and she's right where she needs to be right now.

The first quality to concentrate on is confidence. Merriam-Webster defines it as "a feeling or consciousness of one's powers or of reliance on one's circumstances." For us, it's important to know that your child doesn't have any right now, on his first day of training.

Luckily, kids warm up to new activities faster than us grown-ups, but please realize that this new environment and funny clothing is different. Imagine walking into your first line-dancing class, seeing all the people, hearing the music, and not knowing what to do.

> **Confidence is the cornerstone of martial arts training.**

This phase is *delicate*. Your child's confidence will be built carefully at first, and with good reason. Confidence is the cornerstone of martial arts training. Perfect technique and impeccable focus aren't important yet, because none of that can happen without a solid foundation of confidence.

Just as high-rise buildings must be constructed on solid ground, everything that martial arts training imparts—respect, self-control, fitness—comes after a solid brickwork of self-esteem is laid down.

I'm not talking Bruce Lee-swagger here. Your child needs to feel that this new world is safe, fun, and accepting. Many kids brought to the dojo are there for important reasons—bullying, peer-pressure, poor self-image—things that might make them wary of new experiences. A good dojo is an accepting one.

Many years ago, a mother brought her son to my dojo for his first introductory class.

> *"Can you tell me about James and what might make him a good martial arts student?"* I asked.
>
> Mom: *"Uh, well... he doesn't listen. His teachers say he's a total class clown. Grades are slipping-"*
>
> *"Okay, but can you tell me some good stuff?"*
>
> Mom: *"I guess he's good at skateboarding. But he never listens to me, just does whatever he wants..."*

All of this with James' impressionable nine-year-old ears tuned in the whole time. No wonder he was acting out. The most trustworthy people in his world—parents and teachers—had labeled him a troublemaker. He simply believed them and walked the talk.

Damaging? Yes. Heartbreaking? Totally. Common? Unfortunately. It's hard to see a child come to our dojo, already crushed under years of negative expectations.

You can bet I made absolute sure that James was never given the chance to bring the troublemaker identity with him into the dojo. From day one, I pointed out every instance of discipline and focus he exhibited. Predictably (to me, anyway), the class clown never emerged. Like most troublemakers, James was very bright and highly receptive to attention—in this case, positive attention. He went on to become a great role model and class leader.

As you can see, your child needs confidence first—to step onto the floor, to join in, to start something new. She needs to be given the chance to form her own dojo identity, one perhaps different from how she's treated everywhere else. She needs encouragement. A good instructor will ease her into class and keep it positive. But even the best instructor needs your help. The Sensei Secrets below are some ways you can build your little white belt's confidence early.

White belt is an exciting time, but a delicate one. Most Sensei agree that the highest drop-out rate is within the first few months, so take some time, do it right, and give your young Power Ranger the confidence he needs!

Now that a strong foundation is forming, let's think about the first thing to build on top of it...

SENSEI SECRETS

6 WAYS TO CREATE CONFIDENCE

1. Praise them after every class. Be specific and sincere. "Your kicks were very high today" or "Nice job listening to your instructor!" Being specific means you have to be there and watching class.

2. High-five! A physical demonstration of your approval!

3. Keep it positive. Ask what their favorite parts of class were and why. Tell them what your favorite parts were too.

4. Ignore. Turn a blind eye to anything less than satisfactory. This isn't always easy, but you have to give your child a chance to build on success so don't criticize too early!

5. Help them! Practice a little at home, teach them to tie their own belt, and take pictures!

6. Reroute! Even kids can be self-critical sometimes. When this happens, point out the good things they did in class and remind them that everyone has challenges. Martial artists simply don't give up!

3 YELLOW BELT

RESPECT

Respect is an extremely important virtue within the martial arts. Our dojo definition of respect is "treating others with kindness and courtesy." It is the bedrock of the relationship between you and your Sensei and, in a properly organized dojo, between all students. Without respect, the martial arts are just fighting techniques. Every communication within the school should be respectful.

For kids, *black belt respect* comes in three forms:

1. The Bow. Whether you train at a Kung Fu kwoon, Tae Kwon Do dojang, or Karate dojo, bowing is important. At most schools, you will bow onto and off of the mat, as well as to your instructor and partners throughout the session. The bow is a physical acknowledgement of respect to the practice of martial arts.

2. Protocol. The use of titles and formality can differ from studio to studio, so make sure you know the etiquette of your particular dojo. Sensei, Master, Mr. or Mrs. for instructors, Yes Ma'am/No Ma'am—all of these are used. Once your child understands the rules, help them turn them into habits—and, importantly, observe the titles yourself. It's confusing for your child to hear you refer to their Sensei as "Hey Mike," yet be expected to maintain protocol themselves.

3. Listening. I'm sure you agree, listening is critical to any display of respect, inside or outside of training. Your child's instructor will expect him to hold still and be attentive in class—

> **Without respect, the martial arts are just fighting techniques.**

and, with time, become a great listener in other aspects of his life.

If you enrolled your child in martial arts specifically to work on respect, you can expect it to be awhile before it begins to manifest outside the school. We're talking about shaping your child's character here, and change won't happen instantaneously. But with enough practice, it can become habit!

One of the things we do in my school is to ask parents if their child has used *black belt excellence* outside of the dojo. This is a chance for Mom and Dad to reinforce the positive habits they want to see at home and school.

At the end of class, we ask for evidence of these victories. Typically, we're bombarded with news:

> *"Matthew helped his sister clean her room without being asked."*

> *"Hannah has been working on listening, and today she did everything her mom asked her to do without a fight."*

And so on. Everyone claps and high-fives. It's a great chance to publicly acknowledge effort and respect. To make it even better, kids who display *black belt excellence* at home are awarded with special stripes on their belt as yet another reinforcement.

Here's how you can help support the lessons of respect your child is learning in the dojo...

SENSEI SECRETS

4 WAYS TO REINFORCE RESPECT

1. In the loop. If your academy does not offer *black belt excellence* reports at the end of class, speak to the instructor before or after class (or email them) to let them know about your child's victory. Often, they'll take the time to congratulate them for their hard work.

2. Blind eye. Try to ignore or downplay small episodes of disrespect at home... but when they do something right—no matter how small—bring it up! "I like how you were just now being a great listener." Only award attention to behaviors you want to see repeated!

3. Invoke the Sensei. Of course, it's unrealistic to expect your child to magically become perfectly respectful. When moments of disrespect occur, try this: "What would Sensei think of this? Are you showing *black belt respect*?" It's not exactly a threat to report their behavior to the Sensei... but it often makes them stop and think. At my school, instructors are more than happy to call a child at home to ask if they're showing *black belt respect*, if Mom or Dad asks for it.

4. Set the example. This one is super important. No amount of martial arts training will instill an attitude of respect in your child if they aren't seeing you practice it first. You know how absorbent children can be, and they will follow your example no matter what. So make sure it's a good one!

Lastly, a note about dojo protocol and respect. Please—*please*—let the Sensei teach. Do not coach from the sidelines. Even if your child is struggling or not performing up to your standard, let the Sensei handle it. To speak out during class is disrespectful, distracting and, worse, undermines the instructor in the eyes of your child, making their job much harder.

Secondly, if there is a seating section in your school, use it to spectate from. It's not a conversation area (unless it's walled-off). Loud conversation disrupts the class, and there is no place for distraction in a dojo!

No martial art can be taught or learned without respect. But what if your young student isn't the poster-child of virtue yet?...

4 SENSEI SECRET

THE ROLE OF PUNISHMENT

Times have changed.

You may be lucky enough to have done martial arts as a kid. In the seventies and eighties, the martial arts were exploding in America, thanks to Hollywood.

Back then, martial arts training was rough. Many instructors had studied in Asia while stationed at military bases—or had trained under someone who had. In keeping with the military environment, discipline was strictly and harshly enforced. If you trained during those times, you probably have stories.

My first introduction to martial arts was in 1989. I was a little overweight, bespectacled, and getting picked on in school. Mom suggested Karate and I was psyched! My very first class was one-on-one.

The adult instructor threw front kicks at me for about five minutes while I blocked. My twelve-year-old forearms connected against his shinbone over and over, until they were black and blue. It hurt, but I thought "This is Karate!" It was actually hazing.

A few weeks later, the class was told that if we didn't squeeze our fists tight, we were going outside on the asphalt for knuckle pushups. Some kids didn't squeeze, and there were tears. I made sure not to be one of them.

> **Character quality is grown through self-image.**

I think my mom saw it as an opportunity to discontinue classes, a few months later, when I sprained my ankle.

I didn't start again until 1992, at the age of fourteen. This new academy was better, more professional. Still, I can clearly remember my very first visit to the dojang (Korean word for dojo). I watched a young instructor put an eight-year-old in knuckle pushup position on the hardwood floor for ten minutes for joking in class. Tears started around minute two, sobbing around the fourth.

Did he learn his lesson? Probably. But he also learned that Karate isn't cool! He didn't stay much longer and the positive benefits of martial arts were lost to him.

I believe that punishment has its place in the dojo—but it's rare, and only employed when the bad behavior affects other students. It earns a quiet ushering off the mat, time out, and speaking to after class. If it continues, stripes and belts can be upheld.

No one gets knuckle pushups.

No one gets screamed at.

I've had parents question my reluctance to employ punishment in classes. My defense is simple: character quality is grown through self-image.

As mentioned in chapter one, the troublemaker identity is given no oxygen inside the dojo. With enough positive reinforcement, it shrinks away to nothing—leaving only room for success.

If a child is called out, reprimanded in front of everyone, and assigned a punishment, he's getting attention (which he wants, good or bad) and having his troublemaker identity publicly strengthened. The dojo has become just another place where he's viewed as difficult and the cycle continues.

In a good school, you may be surprised when a child is allowed to lose focus or drift a little bit. Don't think it's going unnoticed. The Sensei is waiting for the right moment to reel them back in. That moment is the very first second the child shows anything resembling focus.

> "Everyone stop! I want to take a moment and point out Jake's focus. Watch how he's looking straight ahead, holding still, and listening. Give him a hand! High five!"

Jake is suddenly the model of focus. He's holding himself up confidently, basking in the glory. He loves the spotlight and now *wants* to focus.

This way, Jake's behavior is corrected and he begins to internalize the skill of focus.

In short, public punishment is effective in the short term but very counterproductive in the long term. Martial arts training is very much a long term activity.

The good Sensei is patient, waiting for her moment—and so is the black belt parent!

We're starting to understand how behavior is molded within the walls of the dojo. Confidence is followed by respect, with a healthy dash of...

5 ORANGE BELT

SELF-CONTROL

Self-Control can mean different things at different ages.

With young ones, my martial arts definition of self-control is "Keeping your hands to yourself, even when you're upset or angry." For an older child, it's "the skill of controlling your own behavior."

Either way, I'm sure you'd agree that the skill of impulse control at a young age is critical. A child who learns to make healthy decisions will carry that ability into adulthood.

Luckily, self-control is an essential tenet of martial arts training. From day one, your child hears that these techniques are for self-defense, only to be used if truly threatened. Even then, they are coached to use restraint and only do enough to leave the situation safely. Your Sensei will make it clear that students who use Karate to bully others may no longer attend classes.

As parents, we're also concerned about other aspects of self-control. Today's children face threatening statistics: an epidemic of obesity, a meteoric rise in childhood diabetes, and a constant barrage of junk food marketing. It's never been more difficult to make healthy choices, or more crucial.

Instructors first teach self-control through partner drills. Sometimes called one-steps or self-defense techniques, these exercises demand physical restraint. A student is taught to throw the punch or kick at full speed but stop at the last instant, so as not to hurt their opponent. This type of drilling is very structured; the child is taught exactly how to move, where to freeze, when to start over. Expectations are clear and every element is rehearsed.

As skill and ability increases, this physical self-control is carried into sparring, or "free fighting." Now the structure is abandoned. Your child has drilled enough to use her moves in a free-flowing format. She must defend, move, and counter against another child—while still using the utmost control of her techniques. Especially with kids, the object of sparring is not to hurt or even hit the opponent; it usually involves scoring points for coming close to the target with speed and accuracy.

These two training methods can be seen as metaphors for self-control practice. At first, the child must be constantly monitored and verbal expectations must be clear. With time, more freedom is earned.

I had a young student named William. At age eight, he had already displayed the warning signs of a wild temper at home. Though he had never gotten physical with another person, he would rage at anything within reach—destroying furniture and even kicking holes in walls. Understandably, Mom and Dad were at their wits end. Telling him to calm down was useless. Punishment made it worse. "I tell him to go punch his pillow, a teddy bear—anything that won't break!" said Mom.

That gave me a flashback. As a kid, I had temper issues also. And my mom said the same thing! Traveling back in time, I remembered how little that advice helped. I was angry! Punching a stupid pillow would not satisfy my pent-up, pre-adolescent rage!

At the end of William's class, I had a talk with him. "Mom says you've been losing your temper at home. It's okay to be angry but not to break things. Remember, a martial artist always needs to show self-control." Great, another lecture from some grown-up who didn't understand.

"So here's what we'll do." I retrieved an old heavy bag that had been at the dojo for years. It was canvas, discolored, duct-taped in places, and hung from rusty chains. In short, it had been well loved throughout the years. "This is my favorite heavy bag. You can take this home. Every time you get angry, I want you to hit this. Put your gloves on first, because this thing will skin your knuckles. But listen, this bag is my favorite. It's still my bag and, if you don't use it, I'm taking it back. Mom will tell me if things are getting broken around the house and I'll come take the bag back. Got it?"

William understood. He insisted on carrying the bag, which easily weighed as much as he did, to the car. He couldn't wait to show his dad what Sensei McShane had entrusted him with.

His temper did not subside quickly, but he used that old heavy bag. When he got frustrated, he'd put on his sparring gloves. That was a cue for Dad to follow him into the basement and even coach him. "Good punch. Give him a kick! Another one! Another one!" When anger surfaced, his outlet was slowly re-routed to something less destructive.

The bag went with William when his family moved away, but it was worth it. I'd like to think it's still hanging in a basement somewhere.

Your child is starting to believe in himself. He's respecting himself and others, while keeping his hands to himself and taking time to contemplate his decisions. Things are starting to come together and, in the dojo, we call this...

SENSEI SECRETS

3 WAYS TO SUPPORT SELF-CONTROL

1. Stop the presses! Even if your child struggles with self-control, there are times when he makes good decisions. When this happens, stop everything and praise him! Gradually, he'll start to identify with thought before action. Be specific: "I liked how you decided to eat an apple instead of chips."

2. When you can't ignore. Self-control is one of those times when you may need to address the negative behavior out-right—especially if it affects other people. "You are sitting out because that's not how a martial artist behaves."

3. Walk the talk. If you are quick to shout or lose your temper, your child will learn more from your actions than your words. Same goes for eating habits!

6 PURPLE BELT

FOCUS

First, let me welcome you to intermediate level! There are unique changes and challenges that will occur at this stage of your young martial artist's growth, as you'll discover in the coming chapters.

In martial arts, focus is defined as "the ability to think about one thing at a time and block out distractions." For older kids, we add "to concentrate your eyes, body, and mind on one point."

The benefits of focus are many. A child who can focus has an easier time at school. They are better listeners at home, able to stay on task and complete chores without being sidetracked. If they play sports, they're better teammates and easier to coach.

In martial arts, focus is serious business. If a lapse in focus occurs—in, say, sparring—the result can be dramatic. When you're honing your hands and feet into weapons, a high level of concentration is much appreciated by your classmates.

Initially, we make focus simple to understand for young students by making it more physical than philosophical. We use the *attention position*.

"Feet together!"

"Hands by your side!"

"Stand straight!"

"Eyes straight ahead!"

I then ask the student to find a spot on the wall to stare at.

"Focus comes in three parts. First, you focus your body by holding perfectly still. Then you focus your eyes by choosing an objective. Once your body and eyes are focused, only then is your mind able to fully concentrate."

Here's a Sensei Secret: For the first few belts, as long as we can keep a child standing still and (somewhat) listening, we're fairly content. Again, every skill in martial arts is acquired incrementally. Some kids are "factory equipped" at age four to be fully focused. Most aren't, and will have a difficult time being completely engaged until older. But if given enough time, everyone gets there.

It's at the intermediate level that an instructor begins to expect real focus. We look for:

Laser beam eyes: Kept straight ahead or on the instructor.

Call and response: "Twist your hips! Twist what?"
"Your hips, Sir!"

Sustained intensity: Consistency of effort in every minute of every class.

Grasp of material: Clearly understanding what's being taught.

Recall: Memorization of combinations, techniques, and more complicated curriculum like katas.

Odds are, if you ask your child what they worked on in class and they're able to answer you in detail, they're beginning to internalize the quality of focus. Even better, they can explain it and display it.

> **It's not easy, but it is simple.**

We've all seen martial arts demonstrations before, and one of the most popular elements of these performances is board breaking. Whether your school offers board breaking or not, it can be a valuable tool for teaching focus (and confidence, and goal-setting, and follow-through, and... you get the point).

The thing about board breaking is, it's simple.

It's not easy, but it is simple.

Here's what I mean: if your technique is correct, and you believe in it enough, and you hit the board in just the right spot, it will work every time. It won't hurt and it will feel effortless.

However, an unfocused punch changes everything. Not enough power, too much power—being off by an inch or two can result in failure. Even if the board breaks, the pain in your hand loudly announces your error in focus.

It's only through coordinating all the elements of a proper technique—body, eyes, mind—that the "effortless" break occurs. Ask any black belt: we all have stories of board breaking gone right and wrong (wrong is usually the more entertaining story). But when it's right, it's right. It's Tiger Woods and Michael Jordan and that guy in the office who always nails the garbage-can longshot. That coordination of elements is focus and it's a place where amazing things can happen, even for young Karate Kids.

SENSEI SECRETS

3 FACTORS OF FOCUS

1. Correction sandwich. Children won't always be focused. One way to get them back on task is what Sensei call "Praise-Correct-Praise." Rather than just pointing out the negative—"You're not listening today!"—start by finding something good. "I like how you made your bed this morning all by yourself. Let's see if you can get the rest of your chores done without stopping."

When they get it right, praise them again for showing focus. It's a great way to make corrections without drawing attention to undesired behaviors. *Note:* Avoid the word "but" at all costs! You can see that the message of "I like how you made your bed BUT you're not getting your chores done" is not the same as the above example. *Hint:* substitute the word "now" every time you want to use "but."

2. Speak the language. A lengthy discourse on the virtue of applied focus will not make much headway with a child. But giving them a good "why" can put it in perspective. "When you get off the bus, homework comes first. Now sit down and get it done," may not be as effective as "If you focus on getting your homework done now, the more time you'll have to play outside later." This is not the same as bribery, which sets up an unwanted precedent. Compare the above example to "If you get your homework done, I'll get you an ice cream cone." In the future, your child may not see the purpose for completing homework if there isn't some type of reward.

3. Within earshot. This is subtle and perhaps a little manipulative—let's be honest, parenting requires a degree of manipulation—but can be effective. If you happen to have more than one child, this one can work well. Logan is focusing but Colin isn't. "I like how much you're concentrating right now, Logan. Good work, keep it up!" If Colin overhears, he may just snap into line to get your attention. Once he does, congratulate him on his effort! *Note:* Don't make it a competition, which can set up some yet more unwanted precedents for the future. For instance, avoid saying "Nice job, Logan. Now if only Colin could do the same..."

Are all martial arts created equal? Is one better than another for teaching life skills? Can it be possible that your child is taking the wrong martial art? Let's talk about the different styles of martial arts and what they offer.

7 SENSEI SECRET

REGARDING STYLES

"Kung Fu is the best because that's what Bruce Lee did!"

"Yeah but Chuck Norris does Tang Soo Do!"

"Steven Seagal does Aikido, that's why it's the best!"

"That's why it's the worst!"

The argument over which martial arts style is the best has raged for years. The good news is, as a parent looking for the mental training that martial arts study provides, style doesn't matter much.

No one system lays claim to the ultimate in character education. It's the instructor that matters most when it comes to teaching respect, self-control, and focus through martial arts. More on selecting an instructor later.

There are only two considerations when it comes to style, depending on your preferences.

If the idea of competition interests you and your child, some styles offer more opportunity than others. Tae Kwon Do tends to feature a sporting aspect. So does Judo. Some "Karate" schools (which is a generic term) have tournament teams, some don't. If this option is important to you, make sure to ask the instructor.

How interested are you in self-defense for your child? Some parents don't care at all about fighting ability, and some prioritize it. Neither is wrong, but just understand that in practical self-defense, not all styles are created equal.

This is where it gets tricky, because every martial arts school in America advertises self-defense—and most instructors believe that their style is effective in this regard. If you call every dojo in your area and ask if self-defense is a big part of their training, *they will all say yes!* Having been involved with martial arts as long as I have, I can't agree.

Many styles taught in America focus more on the "art" than the "martial." There is nothing wrong with this—many instructors want to preserve the time-honored traditions of their system—but there is also nothing particularly artistic about real self-defense. For a child to be able to defend herself against a bully—or, worse, an adult—a real emphasis must be placed on tested defense strategies.

5 SELF-DEFENSE SPECIFIC STYLES

1. KRAV MAGA

Designed for the Israeli military, Krav Maga (meaning "contact combat") is a no-nonsense system emphasizing aggressive reaction, stress management, and fitness. It is comparatively quick to learn (soldiers in Israel learn it in six months or less) and is completely committed to one goal: self-protection. There is nothing artistic about Krav Maga but it is the most effective style I've come across for sheer practicality. It was designed for adults, but there are an increasing number of schools offering it to kids. And despite how intense it looks, it can be taught safely. Just make sure you watch some classes and trust the instructor before enrolling.

Pros:	100% dedicated to self-defense
	Lots of exercise
	Addresses weapons attacks
	Addresses ground-defense, which is important for kids
Cons:	Hard to find kids classes
	May be little or no character component

2. WRESTLING

Useful for self-defense and found in most schools and rec departments, good old-fashioned Wrestling comes with excellent conditioning and mental toughness.

It is a sport and not a self-defense system, but many of the skills learned in Wrestling carry over extremely well to self-protection. I recommend Wrestling as a supplement to other martial arts because it is seasonal.

Pros:	Practical and physical
	Promotes perseverance
	Strong emphasis on sparring
Cons:	100% competition-oriented
	May lack verbalized character lessons
	Can be very rough
	Does not address weapons

3. BRAZILIAN JIU-JITSU (BJJ) and/or JUDO

These grappling styles allow a smaller person to survive and defeat a larger, more aggressive assailant with leverage and timing. They typically involve bringing the fight to the ground, restraining an attacker, and applying chokes or joint locks if necessary. I like it for kids because it does not involve punching or kicking, and a child can use what she knows to end a self-defense situation without even hurting her opponent, if need be. More important, full-resistance sparring can be done in every class, which simulates the feel of real self-defense.

Striking systems cannot offer full-contact sparring nearly as often due to the risk of injury, *and kids shouldn't ever do full-contact striking anyway*. I really like the idea of judo and BJJ for girls. As they age, the types of attacks men and women will face become different.

The emphasis these grappling arts give to escaping being pinned to the ground and fighting against larger, stronger attackers makes them especially effective for women.

Pros: Potentially non-violent
Practical
Safe even at 100% (with good instruction)
Strong sparring emphasis

Cons: Hard to find kids BJJ classes
(Judo is usually more available)
Only good for one-on-one situations
Some schools can be extremely competitive
Probably does not offer weapons defense

Note: Jiu-Jitsu styles are not all the same! There's a big difference between Brazilian Jiu-Jitsu and the Japanese version. Make sure to ask!

---

4. MMA (Proceed with *caution!*)

Mixed Martial Arts is a blend of the most practical techniques from all styles, making it very useful for self-defense. It involves Kickboxing, Wrestling, and Brazilian Jiu-Jitsu elements. However, you must be extremely careful when considering an MMA program for your child.

Schools come in two categories: gyms and dojos. Gyms only exist to produce fighters and usually offer no formal character training. The dojo version is basically a Karate school that teaches a watered-down MMA program.

If you're reading this book you're interested in character training, so the dojo program would be a much better fit. It won't be as hardcore, but it won't be as dangerous either.

Pros:	Practical
	Well rounded
	Plenty of exercise
Cons:	May be too hardcore for kids
	May not feature character training
	Does not offer weapons defense
	Note: Avoid any program that allows kids to spar with full contact.

5. KENPO

Kenpo is closer to what you might consider Karate but places a stronger emphasis on self-defense. The thing to keep in mind is that Kenpo can be a somewhat generic term and different schools specialize in different things. Some schools may be very competitive and offer classical weapons training and jump spin kicks. Some studios are more practically oriented. If self-defense is a concern, ask questions but more importantly, sit and watch. If there's a lot of flash, you may be in the wrong school for your child's needs.

Pros: Kenpo offers a lot of straightforward self-defense
Character training occurs in most studios

Cons: "Sport style" Karate sparring may not be practical
May address weapons defense (but don't include any weapons that Ninja Turtles use as practical!)
Might place a lot of emphasis on areas other than self-defense

---

There are other systems out there that are great for self-defense, but I haven't included them because they are more obscure. If you're not sure about a certain style, do some Google research.

Just remember, *every* instructor in every style claims self-defense proficiency. If you notice certain popular styles are conspicuously absent from my list, it's on purpose.

No matter how effective a style or school claims to be, no program should go so far as to have children spar with full-contact striking—especially if head contact is allowed. Sparring is great for self-defense confidence, but it must be safe and monitored by instructors.

Kids should always wear protective gear and should *never* be instructed to punch each other in the face or head with hard contact. Ask the instructor about how they teach sparring and what is expected.

Again, the character components of martial arts may vastly outweigh effective self-defense when it comes to your situation. Personally, I feel that this type of training is critical for both children and adults (more in the red belt chapter). Either way, remember that though every studio advertises self-defense, not all are equal in this area.

We've done a lot character-building work so far. Things are starting to come together. Wouldn't it be great if your child started to intentionally develop their own focus, respect, and self-control without being asked to? Yes, and it's called...

8 BLUE BELT

SELF-DISCIPLINE

Now we're getting to the good stuff.

Naturally, every child will progress through these steps at different paces. It takes hard work and diligence on both your part and theirs, but given enough attention, the mental aspects of martial arts will start to become habits.

That's because your child is developing *self-discipline*, what martial arts instructors call "doing the right thing without being told."

Notice the distinction here: it's not "discipline," but "self-discipline." What's the difference? A lot. Discipline means having to watch over your child constantly, shaping their every action and forcing them to be responsible.

Self-discipline is hands-free. This is the time when your Karate Kid starts to take responsibility for herself. Maybe it means she practices piano without being told, takes the garbage out, or helps with siblings. Either way, your strict oversight is not as necessary now.

Nice.

This is a fun stage for Karate Parents. I love getting emails saying, "Jaden is night-and-day from when he first started Karate. He's doing everything around the house on his own and getting better grades in school than ever."

> **Self-discipline is the beginning of true confidence.**

Self-discipline makes everything easier. All the previous qualities are starting to come together, and your child knows it.

Self-discipline is the beginning of true confidence. Remember back at white belt, when Jaden needed all that reassurance? The source of his confidence was external. Both you and Sensei had to be very watchful to make sure Jaden was comfortable in class and that his self-esteem was increasing.

Now Jaden feels the confidence coming from within himself. This is a powerful knowledge and it begins to show itself as confidence.

A good Sensei notices self-discipline in the dojo and calls attention to it. As mentioned previously, we catch students doing things right and use that moment to draw everyone's attention.

> *"I noticed that Jaden bowed correctly at the door, put his sparring gear bag away, and sat quietly on the mat waiting for class to start—and did all of this without being told. What's it called when you do the right thing without being told? That's right, self-discipline. Let's give Jaden a hand!"*

Want to bet that Jaden will continue doing this in the future, without being told?

An interesting thing happens in the dojo when a child starts to routinely demonstrate self-discipline. The instructor may actually appear to be paying less attention to that child. Notice I said "appear"—because a good Sensei sees everyone and everything that happens on the floor.

It's just that now the "hand-holding" phase of your child's martial arts career is ending. He's becoming a real student, active in his own development. Sensei is allowing him a little space to grow into the next phase, which is "role model." More on this later. Just remember, the instructor is not ignoring your child. He's trusting him.

I walked into a store a few years ago. Someone called my name, and when I turned around it was a vaguely familiar young man. He introduced himself as one of my former students from years prior. I hadn't fully recognized him at first. Jon was in his early twenties now but I had taught him when he was twelve. In fact, he was now older than I had been when I was teaching him.

As we caught up, he mentioned he was about to finish college, and how the self-discipline he'd learned in martial arts had been instrumental in getting him through school. He said he'd never forgotten one particular thing I'd said in class about responsibility and those words had come back to him time and again during his studies. We shook hands and parted ways.

I was grateful to hear the impact my class had on him—but the more interesting fact? He'd only gotten to orange belt. It's not like he'd absorbed five-plus years of martial arts philosophy and earned his black belt. He'd only trained for nine months or less.

Martial arts lessons can be powerful, and can stay with young students a long time.

SENSEI SECRETS

4 STEPS TO SELF-DISCIPLINE

1. Be clear on expectations. The dojo is a very organized and structured environment, and a student's responsibilities will constantly be communicated to him. Are your child's home responsibilities as clearly spelled out for him? Is there a list of tasks to be done every day?

2. Start small. You understand the importance of catching them doing something right—but don't wait for surgical spotlessness in their bedroom before you acknowledge their effort. The very minute they put the first toy back in its place, let them know how you feel about it!

3. Don't let up on positive feedback. The more self-reliant your Karate Kid becomes, the less you'll have to monitor him, but don't shut off the praise-faucet. He still needs your approval and wants to be noticed for hard work!

4. Give space. Watch from a distance. Your child, given some freedom, will often make good decisions for himself. He'll need course-correction occasionally, but give him the chance to make you proud!

9 GREEN BELT

PERSEVERANCE

Your child is deep in the intermediate ranks now. Congratulations! In many dojos, green belt is approximately halfway to black belt.

An important lesson to absorb at the intermediate level is perseverance. Our dojo-definition for perseverance is staying strong despite difficulty or delay. It means fighting through challenges or obstacles that may come our way. On the path to black belt, there are many.

The martial arts teach perseverance in a number of ways: the physical hardship of training, the mental challenge of embodying the codes of a black belt.

The ability to persevere yields lifelong benefits. A child who learns persistence will carry that mental fortitude into any difficulty she faces. As adults, we know that the challenges of life do not diminish as we get older. Academics, career, relationships, health—as our obstacles grow, our ability to persevere through hard times needs to be solid.

I chose green belt level to discuss perseverance because of something I call "The Green Belt Blues."

As I mentioned, green belt is about halfway to black belt. Your child has been training for a while now, certainly more than a year, and some of the novelty of martial arts has worn off. Remember white belt, when every class was exciting and fun? Like

**Giving up is also a habit.**

any other activity, that initial sparkle wears off. It's still fun; it just isn't new anymore.

And the black belt, to a child, still seems like a long way off. Think about it: if you're eight, three more years is _forever_. You want to be a black belt, but it's taking so long.

It's not uncommon for Karate Kids to fall into a lull right around green belt. The excitement is forgotten, Karate is now routine, and black belt is distant. It's natural that a sense of malaise can creep in. Even for a young child, these are the "teenage years" of their martial arts experience.

Because this is such a sensitive time, we have to be careful. As parents, we know this is a phase and that martial arts training is truly helping your child grow. You don't want them to give up on something they've invested so much time in, but you don't want them to be miserable either.

This is where perseverance is created. In the dojo, inner-strength is not only manifested through repeated physical struggle; sometimes the fight is against something more mundane and common. Maybe it's... boredom? Maybe it's nice weather and wanting to be outside with friends? Video games? Internet?

As you've read so far, all the mental components necessary for martial arts success—confidence, self-discipline, focus—are habits. They're practiced and performed until they are part of us.

But the opposite is also true. Giving up is also a habit.

Giving in.

Quitting.

It was surprising, the first time a mom brought her six-year-old son for his first class and said "He starts things but always quits. He's already quit soccer, t-ball, and swimming. We're just hoping that Karate is what he likes." I actually hear this all the time now. It's natural for kids to have preferences and to gravitate to certain interests. But I wonder what lesson is being taught when a child is allowed to start and quit every activity. Does it send the message that when we don't like doing something, we can simply abandon it?

Like school?

Like work?

Like marriage?

I joined soccer when I was eight. I was shy, introverted, artistic—but not remotely athletic. I remember my mother saying "If you join, you have to stay with it for the whole season. Are you sure this is what you want?"

Yes, I wanted to play soccer. Sign me up.

By the third practice, I was in tears before we even got in the car. Protesting, bargaining, pleading—I tried it all. No, said Mom. I had made a commitment to the team. I had another two months of practice and games, no debating.

I'd like to say that the lesson was learned and I went on to actually enjoy soccer, but I can't. It was awful. It was as hard for my parents to watch as it was for me to play. I hated it, every minute. But, yes, I did come away with an understanding of commitment and responsibility. Wasn't fun, but thirty-some years later, I'm grateful that the message of perseverance stuck with me.

An even better story occurred at my dojo. A young student—we'll call him Brian—was invited to test for his black belt. He'd started young, and was now a seasoned red belt at the age of ten.

Black belt testing at my school is no joke. It's a ninety-day process involving formal tests, memorization, grueling workouts, thousands of pushups, running, and sparring. It's an intense time for students, instructors, and parents—who are required to coach their young black belt candidates. It is not uncommon for kids to fail their first attempt at black belt testing.

Brian had been training for five years. He was a great kid—funny and always smiling—with supportive parents. But martial arts didn't come easy for him. Though physically coordinated, Brian's challenge was focus. He had always struggled to remember his material and would pass his lower-belt tests by the smallest margin. Effort wasn't the problem. It was concentration.

When he was invited to test for black belt, Brian was excited. His parents were too, but also a bit apprehensive. black belt testing requires a lot of memorization and focus.

Testing began. Brian and a few other kids trained together for a month, working on combinations, self-defense techniques, and calisthenics. Candidates are required to do one hundred pushups in five minutes, even kids. Like I said, no joke.

At the first formal test, it became obvious that Brian's issues with focus were persisting. He was slowed down greatly when trying to remember his material. At the end of the three-hour test, I broke it to Mom, Dad, and Brian that the day had not been successful, and that he could try again in five months.

I've had kids train for five years, fail their first attempt at black belt, and quit in frustration the very next day. It's heartbreaking, after all the work they've put in. I sincerely hoped that Brian would stick with it despite this setback.

Fortunately, he was back to class the next day. Though let down, he accepted his results and got back to training. The other kids all went on to pass and earn their black belts.

Five months later, Brian started the process again, this time knowing fully what to expect. He ran; he sweated; he trained at home. Mom and Dad got him to class four times a week to make sure he would succeed this time.

And he did. He got through the first two tests. The only obstacle left was the final, formal test.

Two weeks out, he sprained his ankle. Doctor's orders, no training for a month. I hated to see him sidelined so close to his goal, so we made a major exception and set up another opportunity for him to test one month later.

The day of Brian's test was hard. His ankle had healed, but his performance was not there. He was trying, but it was obvious that this just wasn't his time. Again, I had to give him the news that his test was over; he could start again in three months.

Imagine working so hard for so long with one goal in mind, only to have it not work out. Even as adults, that is serious discouragement. Brian was dejected; his parents were equally disappointed.

> **The hard times are often the most rewarding.**

To add to it, his teammates passed their test and earned their belts.

That's a lot of rejection for anyone, not just a kid.

But on Monday, there he was, back in class. I was overjoyed. This kid wasn't giving up without a fight.

Three months later—an entire year since his first attempt—testing started again. This time, something was different and everyone could tell. Brian was determined. When he trained, he trained hard. The other kids in the test had to keep up with him.

"He wakes me up," his stepdad told me, "dragging me into the garage to hold pads for him before he gets ready for school. I've never seen him like this. I don't want to jinx it, but I think this is his time."

I thought so too, but didn't say so because anything could happen.

When Brian passed his final test, in front of a panel of adult black belts, there was no question. He'd earned that black belt. He was that black belt. No one doubted, even him, that his time had come.

A few days after the test, back to his happy-go-lucky self, Brian came to me. "Sir, I think that if I hadn't failed my first two tests, I could never have passed this one like I did. It's like failing actually made me better."

Can you imagine having that discussion with an eleven-year-old? If there was ever evidence that martial arts teaches kids about life, this was it.

This is a kid who, when he gets older, will not fear failure. He'll apply to colleges without fearing rejection. He won't procrastinate. He won't hesitate to start his own business, because what's the worst that could happen? Failure? Been there, done that. That's a powerful lesson to learn as a kid.

You've heard that kids absorb information like sponges. Martial arts character training is effective because young brains sponge up the lessons learned from years of growing up in the dojo. As you can see, the training is effectively wired into their brains. Determination and perseverance becomes part of them.

Is it also possible that kids can be trained to give up easily? What are the future ramifications of the quitting habit?

If your child is in the motivation rut, this is a perfect opportunity to impart a valuable lesson—that life isn't always fun or exciting, but we can get through the hard times if we're committed.

As Brian would say, the hard times are often the most rewarding.

Remember, there is light at the end of the tunnel. When your child gets past the intermediate level, he's coming close to black belt. We'll talk about that soon, but let's first discuss the belt system itself. Did you know that belts weren't always a part of martial arts?

SENSEI SECRETS
5 PERSEVERANCE-ENHANCING TIPS

1. Be strong... Your child will test your commitment. If they resist coming to class and you allow it, they've learned you can be bargained with. This makes taking them to Karate much harder in the future and sets up a dangerous precedent.

2. ...But be organized. I recommend getting a Karate Calendar for your child's room. Every Karate day is tagged with a huge "K." In the morning, she knows there's no fighting about video games or playing with friends. It's a Karate Day, period!

3. Private classes. Sometimes a student just needs more one-on-one attention to reignite them. Speak to your instructor about setting up a few half-hour private classes to get re-motivated. Most schools do charge extra for private training but it's always worth it.

4. Train. If you train, you're an even stronger support for your child. The students who stay with martial arts the longest are the ones whose family members are also involved.

5. Persevere yourself! It's not fun to contend with a child who refuses to come to class. But just as my mom taught me perse-verance by making me stick with soccer, you can also set that example for your child. We've all heard our own parents say "Because I'm your parent and I know what's best." Admit it, they were right. And now, so are you!

10 SENSEI SECRET

REGARDING BELTS

Belts are a big part of martial arts training in America. Tell someone that you train and their first question is "What belt are you?"

You might be surprised to learn that belts weren't always a part of the martial arts tradition. In fact, the use of belts to denote rank is only about one-hundred-thirty years old. Jigoro Kano, the founder of Judo, awarded the first black belt in the 1880s to signify expert level. Colored belts didn't come around for another twenty or thirty years.

(Interestingly, the idea for black belts occurred to Dr. Kano after he witnessed top-rated Olympic swimmers wearing black bands to signify their expert status. The tradition of martial arts belts originated from competitive swimming!)

Regardless of their history, belts are important. They do far more than just symbolize rank and experience. They reward hard work, discipline, and effort. More important, they teach all the fundamentals of goal setting.

Many experts agree that there are a number of steps to effective goal setting. The martial arts belt system embodies these steps.

SENSEI SECRETS

6 BELT SYSTEM GOAL-SETTING STEPS

1. Be clear. Know exactly what your long-term goal is. Be specific. In martial arts, the goal is black belt. Just ask any five-year-old boy.

2. Break it down. Set short-term goals on your path. Small, bite-size achievements help build momentum and keep you on track. In martial arts, these short-term goals are stripes and colored belts.

3. Have a deadline. Though you can never pinpoint the date your child will test for black belt, most schools offer stripe and belt testing at specific intervals, usually one month per stripe and three to six months per belt. Use this to approximate a future test date, but allow for flexibility.

4. Find out what you need. To earn belts, you must memorize and perform specific requirements at each level. Typically, your teacher spells out these expectations.

5. Find a coach. Your Sensei!

6. Course correct. You cannot always expect smooth sailing, so use any setbacks to get you back on course!

This is a great way to break down the journey to black belt, but don't forget—we're building habits. Would your child benefit from learning to use this formula for every worthwhile goal in life? Whether saving up for a first car, getting a scholarship, or starting a business, a firm grasp of goal setting is a valuable skill.

Don't let this lesson pass your Karate Kid by. Children can be excited about belts but may not absorb the goal-setting strategies they're practicing. Take time to verbalize it; it's worth it.

A final point on belts, and an important one.

Belts and stripes are symbols of progress. They aren't *actual* progress. The goal isn't the belt; it's what you've done and become to get there.

Sometimes, I see students or parents get too focused on the belt rather than the qualities it takes to earn the belt. This isn't sports—there's no winning or losing. Belts are signposts on the road showing how far you've come. If your child fails in earning a belt, they simply haven't walked far enough yet.

Don't compare your child to anyone else. Some travelers on the road walk fast, some walk more slowly. Occasionally, I hear "Jeremy is a red belt but my green belt son kicks better than him." or "I see white belts with better technique than my orange belt daughter." Both of these statements are unfair because martial arts training is an individual pursuit. Trust your Sensei—they've been doing this a long time. We can sense a child's Karate potential and know if he's living up to it.

Belts are a great feature of martial arts training and a perfect lesson on goal setting—but are ultimately an indicator of personal growth, not the goal itself!

Warning: big changes ahead! Your child is about to step out of the intermediate ranks and into the fast-moving world of advanced training. In preparation for that future black belt test, there are two things every candidate needs, and one is...

11 BROWN BELT

FITNESS

In some schools, brown belt is the last belt before black. In others, it's second to last. Either way, your child is now considered advanced!

That means they have a firm grasp of all the material leading up to this point, and an ability to perform it. The lessons of martial arts, both physical and mental, have been practiced many times.

I'm going to use brown belt level to talk about fitness. All dojos are different; some have fitness requirements and some do not. Either way, I'm sure your child's fitness level is important to you.

All martial artists should be in shape. From a practical standpoint, you need to be able to move quickly in the chaos of real self-defense situations. You may know hundreds of moves, but if you're too fatigued or immobile to use them, they're useless.

More importantly, training in martial arts requires a dedication to your own development. So far, this book has been about the mental aspects of training—but there is no separation between the mental and the physical.

A focused martial artist concentrates on all-around fitness.

A disciplined martial artist commits to a healthy lifestyle.

A self-controlled martial artist doesn't view ice cream as dinner.

And so on.

> **Your physical state is a result of the state of your mental training.**

In short, your physical state is a result of the state of your mental training. You can't be living the black belt lifestyle if health isn't a priority.

The higher you go in the ranks of martial arts, the more you become a role model to others. Living a life of fitness and health sets a great example for those around you.

My Brazilian Jiu-Jitsu teacher is Marcio Stambowsky (google him—seriously). He has a lifelong friend named Alvaro Romano (google him too). The two have trained in BJJ together for over forty years.

Alvaro is in his late-fifties now. A small, friendly, and energetic man, Alvaro moves better than anyone I've ever seen in his age group. Years ago, he developed a program called Ginastica Natural, an exercise system combining the movements of Brazilian Jiu-Jitsu, yoga, and bodyweight exercise. He travels the world now, teaching his techniques at seminars.

Committing to a life of fitness has paid off big for Alvaro. His energy is contagious. He smiles a lot. He can touch his toes, hit a full-split, and knows more pull-up variations than I can count. Fitness is simply part of who he is; it's his life. Approaching sixty, when most Americans have resigned themselves to relative inactivity, he shows no signs of slowing down. He's very inspiring to watch.

My Krav Maga teacher Paul Garcia is the same way. He insists that "the older I get, the better I get" and could easily be mistaken for ten years younger than he is.

This is the way of martial arts, and the younger it's learned, the better.

Let's look at two types of adults that join my school.

One, mid-forties, tells me it's time to get in shape because their "doctor says so." They admit to never having exercised before.

The other, same age, admits to having been lazy about exercise for about ten years, but was fitness conscious earlier in life.

Though both are substantially out of shape, the second student is always more coordinated, less prone to discouragement, and quicker to see results. This doesn't mean the first student is a lost cause, but it's always more difficult for them. Though childhood fitness can accumulate rust if left unattended, the habit is there and is easier to develop than for someone who never worked out.

That's why it's so important for kids to find some type of exercise that they like and that keeps them moving. Luckily for your child, that avenue is martial arts training.

Believe it or not, many martial arts systems are not high-intensity physical activities. It's sometimes possible to study for years but not improve your physical condition appreciably. If this is the case at your school, your child may need to cross-train in another activity to supplement their martial arts.

Help your child develop an interest in physical fitness. It's a habit that can last a lifetime.

SENSEI SECRETS
4 FITNESS RECOMMENDATIONS

1. Set the example. This is #1, no matter what! Your child absorbs your behaviors more than anyone else in their life. It's a responsibility—live up to it!

2. Eat right. Many adults harbor the misconception that enough exercise will produce fitness, regardless of diet. However, many experts agree that up to 80% of your health is dictated by diet compared to 20% by exercise. What's your child eating?

3. Set fitness goals. If your dojo doesn't require them, come up with some for your child. Go online and do some reading about realistic fitness goals for your child's age group. But—and this is important—keep it fun. Challenge, don't enforce. We don't want your child resenting exercise.

4. Train! Do it with them! It's way more fun and you take care of the previous three suggestions in one swoop!

Is it getting warm in here? Things are starting to heat up! Your child is about to make the last step before the legendary black belt. She can focus, act with self-discipline and respect, and is in great shape.

But can she fight her way out of a paper bag? Is this even important? The answer is yes, and find out why as we dig into...

12 RED BELT

SELF-DEFENSE

Here we are—the final colored belt. Red belt means you've now been taught everything you'll need to know to test for black belt.

All of the important mental components of training have been addressed, and the physical requirements have been spelled out.

But can your child take all the techniques he's learned, put them together, and use them to effectively defend himself? black belts, beyond exemplifying the disciplines of the dojo, should be able to hold their own if the need arises. The martial arts, after all, were originally developed for self-protection

As with everything we've worked on so far in this book, self-defense is something best learned young. Judging from applications parents fill out when enrolling their kids at my school, they agree. Self-defense is always among the top priorities.

"I feel everyone needs to know two things," says Master Paul Garcia, my Krav Maga teacher. "how to swim and how to defend themselves."

I agree. It's almost like carrying insurance. You don't like the idea of having to use it, but when you need it, you're sure glad you've got it.

You can greatly diminish the possibility of encountering violence by being smart about where you go and who you're with.

You can practice awareness. But sometimes, violence happens and you need to be prepared.

I'm a big advocate for kids learning real, applicable self-defense. Depending on who you are and where you live, you may not feel as strongly, but hear me out.

In the first chapter, I talked about the importance of confidence—how your child needs to build it first, before anything else can fall into place. Confidence is the concrete under the dojo floor and without it, there would be no dojo.

There is almost nothing that can shatter that concrete faster than being physically dominated by another person. Ask any victim of a violent encounter—it changes everything. It affects how you view the world and, more importantly, how you view yourself. Physical bruises fade quickly, but self-esteem and confidence sustain damage that can last for years.

Kids learn quickly. And being physically abused—even by another child—can quickly teach them that the world is a dangerous, scary place that they are powerless against.

I'm not just talking about violent, dangerous encounters. The bullying that has always been commonplace in grade schools (sometimes even labeled a rite of passage!) is entirely complicit in the undermining of confidence and self-worth.

Conversely, kids who know—*know*—they can defend themselves grow into adults who know the same. The boy who stood up for himself and stopped bullying dead in its tracks becomes a teenager who doesn't bend to peer-pressure, and a man who isn't intimidated. To the college girl who's fought and held her own against boys in dojo matches for years, no means no.

I'm talking about real self-defense. As mentioned earlier in the chapter on styles, some systems prioritize it and some don't. I believe for a child—or anyone—to be truly confident in their abilities, they have to spar. They have to face resistance. They need to

The boy who stood up for himself becomes a man who isn't intimidated.

contend against someone trying to pin them to the floor, or punch them, or tackle them. All of this can be done safely under the eye of a good instructor, and it should be eased into gradually, but there's no replacement for this kind of training.

The more a student gets familiar with the pressure of a fully resisting opponent, the less she fears it. She can, in an instant, assess a threat and say, "there's nothing you can do to me that I haven't faced in the dojo a hundred times." That's self-defense confidence.

An interesting thing happens when a child develops self-defense confidence. Often, without ever having to fight or stand up for themselves, bullies simply avoid them in the first place.

The "Shark Analogy" is particularly helpful. Sharks are known to have an acute ability to sense prey. They can smell blood from long distances. They are drawn to helpless thrashing.

Bullies are similar. They have an innate ability to spot victims. I read a study years ago where a team of researchers interviewed violent criminals about target selection. Many said that they could spot a potential victim from a distance, based on subtle cues such as body language, posture, and eye contact. And they could do it in an instant. In another test, they were shown a video of a roomful of people and asked to point out the easiest victims. Most answered instantly, and were able to give reasons. When compared, many of these criminals had chosen the same targets.

What sharks, criminals, and bullies can sense is vulnerability, panic, and opportunity. The schoolyard thug is not looking for a challenge. He simply feels strong by making others feel weak. For that reason, he seeks out easy targets.

A child who knows he can defend himself does not emanate signals of doubt or panic. They may walk a little taller or respond more assertively, but something imperceptible to most of us announces, "I'm not a victim." When the bully scans the room, a self-assured child is not even a blip on the radar.

Early in my career, my youngest student was a three-year old boy. Nicholas was very talented for his age and always excelled in classes. By the age of five, he was competing in tournaments. By seven, he was winning regional and national competitions. His talent was very exceptional.

Neither of Nicholas's parents was very big and, as he got older, he didn't grow as fast as others his age. In the dojo, he often found himself facing kids almost twice his size. But what he lacked in stature, he made up for in tenacity and sheer skill. The kid could move, and I saw him conquer many larger opponents.

By the time Nicholas entered high school, he was about the size of the average fifth or sixth grader, baby-face and all. As you know, high school can be a rough place for anyone who is different; too small, too big... too anything. I knew Nicholas could protect himself, but I wondered what would happen.

I caught up with his dad about six months into Nicholas's freshmen year and asked him what his high school experience had been like so far. Specifically, had he been picked on?

"You know what? No. Never happened. And the funny thing is, nobody even knows he's a black belt. Trouble just never comes his way."

Something about the way Nicholas carried himself communicated that he was not an attractive target. Others could sense his self-assurance. Because Nicholas wasn't afraid to fight, he never had to.

Being able to rely on your own abilities is a powerful feeling, especially for kids growing up in an uncertain world. Learning to protect yourself guards against the negative effects of abuse, bullying, and violence.

As a parent, would you feel better knowing that your child was trained to respond against and escape from physical attack? Of course! That's why self-defense training is so important for kids.

Black belt is just around the corner. As you'll learn, this level is not about secret techniques, expert deadliness, or ninja-like perfection. It's about your child embodying everything they've learned in these last five years. But first, let's talk about the person who will get your child there...

SENSEI SECRETS

5 TIPS FOR THE SELF-DEFENSE MINDED

1. Choose the right program. If self-defense is a priority to you, find the right art for your child using the list in the "Styles" chapter. If your child is already enrolled in a program that you feel does not address this issue enough, you have two options...

2. Get private self-defense instruction. Even if you're at a dojo that focuses more on art than practicality, chances are that your Sensei knows what techniques are the best for self-defense. Approach him and ask for a few private classes geared specifically toward self-protection.

3. Cross-train. If private classes aren't the answer, find a Judo or BJJ school to attend once a week, or sign your child up for after-school Wrestling as a supplement to their regular martial arts classes. These systems are completely different than Karate and are great at building mental toughness and tenacity.

4. Spar. If your school offers extra sparring classes, bring your child to them. This is a chance for your child to test his abilities against a moving, breathing opponent. Tournament-style point sparring is not particularly realistic, but any sparring is better than none.

5. Get some padded targets and work at home. This option is not nearly as favorable as the others, but if you have no other choice, practice with your child at home. Invest in some self-defense DVDs and most importantly—go easy. Self-defense ability takes time and intensity should be raised very gradually.

13 SENSEI SECRET

REGARDING INSTRUCTORS

When I was a kid, I used to argue with my friends over whose Karate teacher was better. Not a better teacher, necessarily; just a tougher, stronger, more mythical warrior.

> *Him: "Mine went to China and did Kung Fu on the Great Wall."*
>
> *Me: "Mine could punch the Great Wall in half."*

I still think I'm right, by the way.

But there are far more important factors when selecting an instructor than how they would fare against Chuck Norris.

In fact, the instructor is by far the most significant consideration for a parent who wants martial arts for their child. You are putting the most cherished person in your life in their hands, to teach and to mold. It's critical to choose the right one.

5 THINGS TO LOOK FOR

1. Likability. This is the deciding factor. Good instructors are down-to-earth, positive, and helpful. Think of the opposite of the bad Sensei in The Karate Kid. You have to feel like you're in the right school with the right teacher. Gut-instinct is often one of the best indicators of a good fit.

2. Role-model worthiness. The best instructors lead by example first. Your child will learn just as much by being around his instructor as he will by taking instruction. Is your potential

Sensei in or out of shape? Happy or depressed? Positive or negative? These are elements to consider.

3. Professionalism. Some dojos are run as clubs, by a Sensei who has a day-job. Others are full-time businesses. Part-time operations may offer good instruction, but my suggestion is to find a professional academy—simply for the fact that a professional instructor, who depends on his ability to service his students, can give all of his effort to his teaching.

Also, because the school is always open, there will be more flexibility to fit your schedule. You will pay more. There will be contracts. But if you find the right instructor, it will be well worth it.

4. Dynamism. A good instructor can teach anyone. They can get on one knee and coach four-year-olds. They can be energetic one minute, laid back the next. They can be demanding drill sergeants when necessary. Effective Sensei are versed in motivation, coaching, and communication—not just martial arts (though they may not be formally educated).

Remarkable teachers are truly complex creatures. Ask around town... impressive Sensei come with impressive recommendations.

5. Character curriculum. Every dojo advertises respect, focus, confidence—but not everyone has an organized way to teach them. Most professional schools don't leave character education to chance, and an instructor will make these disciplines part of every class.

5 THINGS NOT TO WORRY ABOUT

1. Trophies. Personally, I think trophies in the window of a dojo are gaudy, but maybe that's just me. In reality, an instructor's tournament record has as little or nothing to do with his teaching ability. I've known non-competitive black belts who can command a class of fifty children, and world champions who are clueless at leadership. Unless you want your child to be the next world champion, don't worry about competitive achievements.

2. Style. If you find a teacher you like who teaches character, martial arts style is not that important *unless* you really want self-defense training.

3. Age. One of the best children's instructors I ever witnessed was only seventeen, not even out of high school. Kai Blackstar, the most famous instructor of four-and-five year-olds in America, is deep in his fifties.

4. Credited. There is currently no regulation on who can or can't be a martial arts teacher. Instructor status is often certified by martial arts organizations—and, honestly, "Level 4 Instructor Certification from the International Federation of United Tae Kwon Do Academies of America LLC" doesn't (and shouldn't) mean anything to the average consumer. You can find excellent instructors who communicate wonderfully with children that aren't "certified" by anyone.

5. Rank or **Title.** My recommendation for instructor rank is black belt. That's pretty much it. Degree doesn't matter that much. And because someone is a "master," it doesn't mean they're a better teacher than anyone else.

Most studios will start you off with an introductory class. It's a good way to meet the Sensei and see if you click. It may be free or cost twenty dollars, but worth it to make sure they communicate well with your child.

It's also a good idea to watch a class. Even martial arts has its share of "slick salesmen," so watch the group class your child will be entering to make sure that the instructor and school "walk the talk."

Below are some suggestions for after you've selected a school and enrolled your child in classes.

Again, I can't emphasize enough how important it is to simply like and trust a potential instructor. Rank, accolades, and titles are meaningless without rapport. If you don't feel it, it's probably best to look elsewhere!

The parent/instructor relationship is one of teamwork. I've stated many times that martial arts teaches character—but, truthfully, your child's Karate training just reinforces the qualities you teach at home.

You and Sensei should be on the same page, comparing notes, and working in conjunction to shape the life of your child for the better. This requires communication.

As we've learned, the black belt is a culmination of years of sweat, study, and dedication. There's just one more quality needed to solidify everything your child has accomplished so far, and that ingredient is...

SENSEI SECRETS

10 TIPS TO SUCCESS WITH YOUR SENSEI

1. Be patient regarding almost everything!

2. Ask questions! Karate is more complicated than T-ball.

3. Listen! Sensei knows what she's talking about.

4. Be involved and watch your child's classes but...

5. ...Let the teacher teach! Don't coach during class!

6. Trust the Sensei to do their job. If you don't trust them, they shouldn't be working with your child.

7. Don't get too comfortable. This is a formal relationship...

8. ...But it is a relationship. Expect ups and downs and even disagreements and be willing to work through them.

9. Communicate constantly. Don't let assumptions go unspoken and don't engage in rumors. I've seen unfounded rumors do serious damage in dojos. In my school, I've had to release students whose parents engaged in rumors and negativity.

10. Contribute to the positive environment. The dojo is a positive place, period!

14 BLACK BELT

HUMILITY

Your child isn't a child in the world of martial arts anymore. Those years of experience and hard work have paid off. Most dojos require three to five years of training before a student is considered for black belt, and in the life of a child, that's a lot of dedication.

To put it in real numbers—if a child attends class twice a week, every week for five years, that's five-hundred-twenty hours of concentrated study.

He succeeded through those tentative early days, unsure of his place in this strange new environment, and his confidence improved. He practiced respect and, more importantly, understood why. His self-control improved, both in and out of the dojo.

Graduating to the intermediate level, his focus got sharper, helping at home and school. Consciously striving to be better, it all started to come together when he began to discipline himself to do the right things without being reminded. Maybe he even encountered an all-too-common dip in motivation and was stronger for persevering through it.

Now an advanced practitioner, he adopted the discipline of fitness and took an active interest in his own health. And though he would never use his training against someone unless he had to, you know he has what it takes to defend himself if the need arises.

> *The most dangerous, experienced, and knowledgeable martial arts experts are often the most down-to-earth.*

All this accomplishment at such a young age makes your child pretty extraordinary. At even the most professional dojos, only between five and ten white belts in a hundred succeed all the way to black.

Impressive!

I know what you might be thinking. Confidence in one hand, fighting ability in the other—have we created a monster? Could this child use his training to do wrong?

A great dojo has a system for creating successful black belt students of all ages. A critical part of this training is humility—"modesty despite position or ability."

Without this aspect, dojos would literally be ego factories!

It has always amazed me how the most dangerous, experienced, and knowledgeable martial arts experts are often the most down-to-earth. It's as if true black belts—equipped with the quiet confidence of humility—feel no need to advertise their proficiency. I've met some truly skilled individuals that you would never guess were highly trained. They're content to fly under the radar.

Disclaimer: An exception to this rule has emerged in the last twenty years with the popularity of mixed martial arts fighting. Within this sub-genre of martial arts training, bravado is rife.

However, these ego displays are often a product of the entertainment element of MMA—and, remarkably, the competitors who engage in it the most are typically the ones with the least amount of actual dojo training.

There are plenty of examples of high-profile MMA fighters who exemplify the quality of humility.

Bragging is a symptom of inadequacy. Those most eager to boast or show off often suffer from serious doubt in their abilities.

To seasoned black belts, martial arts training is as much a part of them as their personality. It's not something they do, it's simply something they are—so making a display of it seems silly and awkward. Most are content to not even bring the topic up; we've all been subjected to the following statements from those who learn that we're black belts:

"Do you have to register your hands as deadly weapons?" (The answer is no.)

"Could you beat Georges St-Pierre?" (The answer is also no.)

"Who would win, Chuck Norris or Steven Seagal?" (Chuck Norris, even in his seventies.)

"Was Bruce Lee as good as they say?" (Yes.)

"Whoa, looks like I need to be careful around you!" (Actually, we're usually the safest guys in the room to be around.)

"What would you do if I grabbed you like this?" (Please don't ask us this.) *"How about this?"*

"Hi-yah!" (This is super annoying.)

Okay, I went on a tangent, but you get my point. We tend to downplay it.

From a practical standpoint, real black belts also have enough humility to know their limitations. We're not superhuman. If anything, our training has taught us overconfidence is always a mistake.

Humility is taught through the culture of the dojo. If the master instructor is humble, her black belts will be too. If an environment of modesty is cultivated, the mindset will rub off on the students.

The quality of being humble is verbally explained to young students, but it seems the best way to teach it is to live it.

Humility is also the product of sparring. When you face a number of different competitors of different skill levels on a weekly basis, it tends to remind you of your place in the scheme of things. It lets you know what you can do, can't do, and shouldn't do. Bragging and swaggering are two of those "shouldn'ts."

The martial arts offer a system of building a child up, equipping her for life, and helping her believe in herself. Modesty, a characteristic of every true black belt, is what binds these qualities together.

SENSEI SECRETS

4 WAYS TO TEACH HUMILITY

1. Are we in the right place? The number one factor in reinforcing modesty is the environment of the dojo. Does the Sensei embody and encourage humility? Does he personify it? Do the other students?

2. Reminders. "Are you acting with *black belt humility* right now?"

3. Role-modeling. As a senior student, your child has younger eyes following them in the dojo. Remind them that they are setting an example for the younger children and that being humble is part of that example. This way, your Karate Kid feels the acknowledgement of this responsibility without having to brag.

4. Team up. If your child is not exhibiting modesty, speak with the instructor. Most teachers do not want their students showing off or bragging. A good Sensei can address the problem in the most effective manner.

15 SENSEI SECRETS

KEY TAKEAWAYS

We've covered a lot: from your child's first days in the gi, to the creation of a self-reliant black belt. As a martial arts parent, there are a few things to remember.

1. Be involved. Kids whose parents take an active role in their martial arts education stay longer and benefit more from training. The dojo is a community, and your presence means a lot to your child.

2. Keep it positive. This one cannot be emphasized enough. Offer sincere praise for your child's efforts, even (and especially) when there doesn't seem to be much to praise. Complimenting a moment of focus, or a high-five for a particularly good class goes a long way. Negativity is toxic in the dojo, and to your child. Be a good finder; find only good.

3. Set the example. Nearly everything learned in the dojo is taught by example. If you want your child to exhibit respect, show respect. If you want your child to act with self-control, practice it yourself. There's no substitute for a great role model.

4. Train. Be the example for your child. Get out there and train! It's something you'll always be able to share and it's simply more fun for everyone!

5. Cultivate a strong relationship with the Sensei. After all, you're a team whose sole mission is your child's development!

6. Don't compare. The martial arts aren't team sports. There's no gold medal for getting to black belt first. Your child is here to work on herself, and comparison simply isn't fair to anyone.

7. Be patient. This is something I learned from Master Voelker, my first real instructor. "If given enough time, everyone gets it." Some kids pick up martial arts training quickly. For others, it takes years for it to really start clicking. Just remember, martial arts training is a marathon, not a sprint. It's a journey.

16 AND LASTLY...

As parents, we want our children to embody all of the qualities that the martial arts are said to teach. Learning these black belt principles young can lead to a better, more fulfilling life. We want to know that our kids are capable, balanced, and ready to face the world because we can't always be there to watch them.

Martial arts training is a reinforcement for the character qualities you nurture at home. Just being around people who are all striving for improvement can be contagious—but there are things parents can do to make martial arts training even more special. That was the purpose of this book; I hope it helps.

I joined martial arts because of bullying. My mother saw that I was having a hard time and thought that I could use some confidence. To this day, twenty-plus years later, I'm extremely grateful that she did.

Though I had dabbled earlier with some other studios and styles, I found my home at Middlesex Tang Soo Do Academy in Old Saybrook, Connecticut at the age of fourteen. A classical, Korean form of Karate, Tang Soo Do emphasizes traditional training methods, forms practice, sparring, and the style's specialty – kicking.

My transformation did not take place instantaneously, or even quickly. As it turned out, there was a lot of work to be done on my self-esteem. I was still uncoordinated. So shy I didn't speak for the first three years, my teachers didn't know what to make of me. But I kept showing up, two to five times a week.

Under the guidance of Master Steven Voelker and his team of instructors, I gradually improved. Tang Soo Do is extremely heavy on repetition, which was a perfect way for me to overcome my awkwardness. I discovered that I was pretty flexible and could do almost any kick they asked me to. I even had some tournament success.

Perseverance paid off. With time, my self-consciousness melted away. When I asked to assist with kids classes, Master Voelker said yes. It turned out that teaching was something I could excel at. The positive feedback I received from students and parents only made me feel more secure. Again, the influence of the dojo environment is powerful.

I realized then that martial arts would be my life. It had changed me. I'd seen it change others too, and it was allowing me—yes, even me—to be a positive influence in the lives of the kids in my classes.

After I earned my black belt in 1996, I became the manager for one of Master Voelker's academies. This is when I really learned to teach and I give all the credit to him for trusting a determined yet green nineteen-year-old kid with his business.

At twenty-four, Master Voelker handed me the keys to one of his academies. The chubby, silent kid from ten years ago was suddenly a businessman. I believe it's the discipline, focus, and perseverance I learned in just ten years of martial arts that allowed me to be successful. The martial arts have given me everything.

Not all kids will become instructors, or even black belts. But given enough time to absorb the culture and character of martial arts training, every child can take those few years of discipline, focus, and respect with them into adulthood—especially if Mom and Dad are right there with them.

In the end, the dojo is simply a wonderful place to grow up.

www.ingramcontent.com/pod-product-compliance
Lightning Source LLC
Chambersburg PA
CBHW050948030426
42339CB00007B/339